Cwm Pennant and Afon Dwyfor

Des Marshall

Gwasg Carreg Gwalch

First published in 2021
© text: Des Marshall
Publication: Gwasg Carreg Gwalch

All rights reserved. No part of this publication
may be reproduced, stored in a retrieval system,
or transmitted in any form or by any means,
electronic, electrostatic, magnetic tape, mechanical,
photocopying, recording, or otherwise, without prior
permission of the authors of the works herein.

ISBN: 978-1-84524-393-7
Cover design: Eleri Owen

Published by Gwasg Carreg Gwalch,
12 Iard yr Orsaf, Llanrwst, Wales LL26 0EH
tel: 01492 642031
email: books@carreg-gwalch.cymru
website: www.carreg-gwalch.cymru

Cwm Pennant and Afon Dwyfor

Contents

INTRODUCTION ... 4

General Map of Eifionydd ... 5

Map of Cwm Pennant ... 7

Map of the Afon Dwyfor ... 9

SECTION 1 - SOURCE TO DOLBENMAEN

1. The source of the Afon Dwyfor ... 12

2. Slate quarries of Cwm Pennant ... 24

Map of the Gorseddau Tramway system ... 31

3. Cwm Ciprwth copper mine ... 32

4. Llanfihangel y Pennant, Brynkir House and Tower ... 38

SECTION 2 - DOLBENMAEN TO LLANYSTUMDWY

5. Dolbenmaen ... 48

6. Burial chambers associated with the area ... 54

7. The middle reaches of the Afon Dwyfor and Llanystumdwy ... 64

SECTION 3 - LLANYSTUMDWY TO THE SEA

8. To the sea ... 76

9. Walks to discover the area ... 84

GLOSSARY ... 88

Introduction

'*Pam, Arglwydd, y gwnaethost Gwm Pennant mor dlws? A bywyd hen fugail mor fyr?*". These are two lines written by the poet Eifion Wyn who grew up in the area taken from his poem 'Cwm Pennant' which has found its way into Welsh folklore. Roughly translated it says: 'O Lord, why did you make Cwm Pennant so beautiful and the life of a shepherd so short?' Cwm Pennant is where revered Tibetan Buddhist teacher Dilgo Khyentse Rinpoche said was a special, sacred place to visit whilst local legends say the people in the valley are intermarried with the tylwyth teg - *fairies*.

Cwm Pennant is one of the most beautiful, totally unspoilt and quietest valleys in Snowdonia. This was not the case when the valley was home to quarrying and mining industries years ago. Then it was a hive of activity and noise resonating from the copper mines at the head of the valley in Cwm Dwyfor and lower down the valley in Cwm Ciprwth to the many slate quarrying enterprises that ranged its whole length. At the head of the valley the remains of the Prince of Wales slate quarry are plain to see and the tramway emanating from the mill below it contouring around the slopes of Moel Hebog into Cwmystradllyn to the main section of the Gorseddau Tramway. This had been built from Gorseddau slate quarry to Porthmadog in 1857 for transporting it's slate from quarry to mill to port. Other slate quarries can also be found. Some just a mere scratching on the surface whilst others such as Moelfre, Isallt and Hendre Ddu much larger. The hustle and bustle of noisy machinery has been replaced by tranquillity and nowadays the only sounds to be heard are the bleating of sheep and birdsong. Picnic tables at the end of the tarmac road up the valley make a grand place to view the magical surroundings. In early spring bluebells on the eastern side here are a most magnificent and colourful sight with the air filled with a wonderful heady scent.

Lower down the valley the ground is fertile but the higher up one travels the more infertile and barren the ground becomes. Rock becomes more evident, having a slight tinge of purple it contrasts strikingly with the tall tracts of bracken. Once across Pont Gyfyng below Craig Gyfyng - *narrow bridge* - the road rises to enter the wilder part of the valley. The

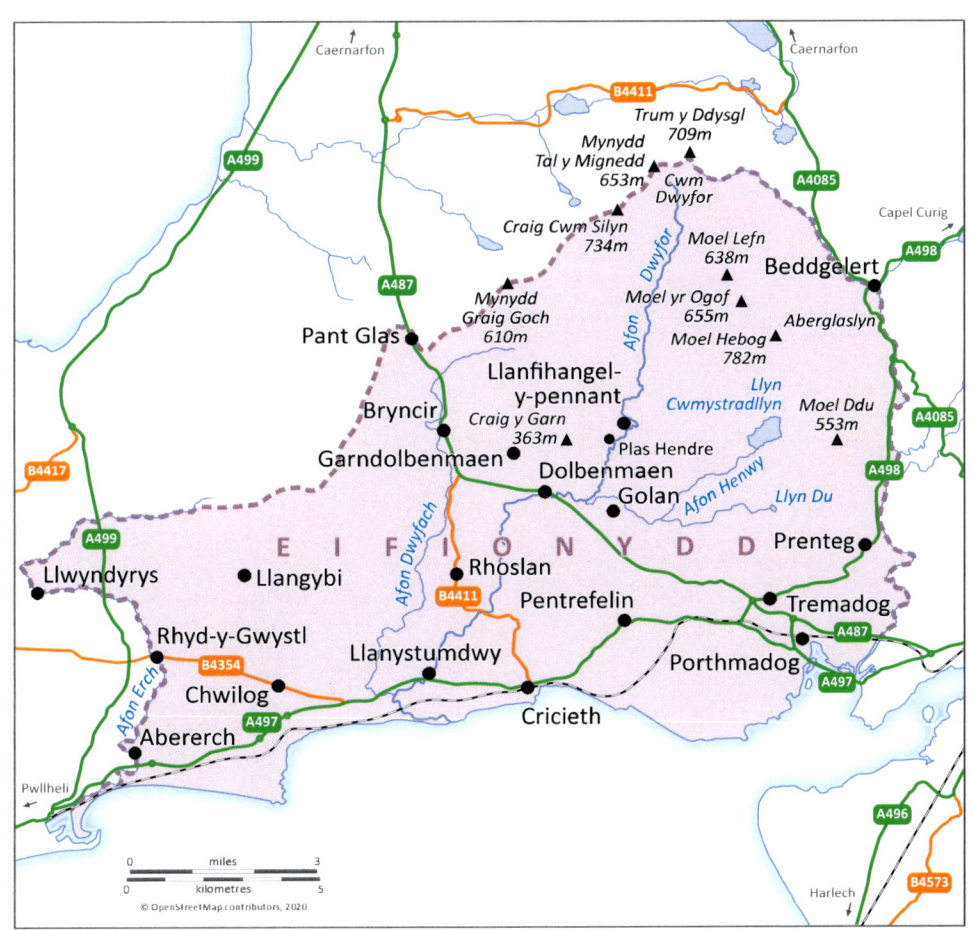

General Map of Eifionydd

huge grassy slopes of Moel Hebog, 782 metres, can be seen soaring up to the right on the east side of the valley with barely a rock in sight. Long walls that rise inexorably to the summit define large fields. To the left of Hebog are the two much craggier mountains of Moel yr Ogof, 655 metres and Moel Lefn 638 metres. It is said that the most famous son of Wales, Owain Glyndwr, hid in a cave on the Beddgelert side of Moel yr Ogof when Wales was retaken by the English. Taking refuge on the mountain he had swum across the Glaslyn at Nantmor, which was then a tidal river, to evade his pursuers. Glyndwr led the last uprising against the English and captured Harlech Castle in 1404. At one time walkers used to start in Cricieth to climb Moel Hebog, a round trip of some 20 miles.

Opposite on the west side of the valley is the fine Nantlle Ridge. This ridge walk/scramble is one of the finest one of its type in Snowdonia. Starting from Rhyd Ddu the traverse continues over seven mountain tops, Y Garn 633 metres, Mynydd Drws-y-Coed 695 metres, Trum y Ddysgl 709 metres, Mynydd Tal-y-Mignedd, Cwm Silyn, Garnedd Goch and the recently added 610 metres summit of Mynydd Graig Goch, to end above Llanllyfni. Incidentally Mynydd Graig Goch became Wales' 190th summit over 610 metres and over in 2008! However, the classic 6 miles traverse ends at Garncdd Goch before descending to the road end above Llanllyfni.

At the lower end of the valley, by the side of the Afon Dwyfor, stands Dolbenmaen a closely knit tiny hamlet. At one time this was on the main stagecoach route from Caernarfon to Porthmadog. Nowadays it is bypassed by the main trunk road, the A487. Plas Dolbenmaen was once an inn that provided beverages to weary travellers as well as a local shop that sold sweets and general supplies that included soap and paraffin. Dolbenmaen was at one time of great strategic importance having a motte and bailey that guarded the fording of the Afon Dwyfor.

The 12½ miles long Afon Dwyfor the river flowing down and through the valley is a pretty one indeed. Starting high up on the slopes of Trum y Ddysgl the tumbling steep start is replaced by slow, tree lined, meanderings down to the sea reaching it a mile or so from Cricieth. The source, close to a wall, is hardly anything at all but the stream quickly swells due to numerous

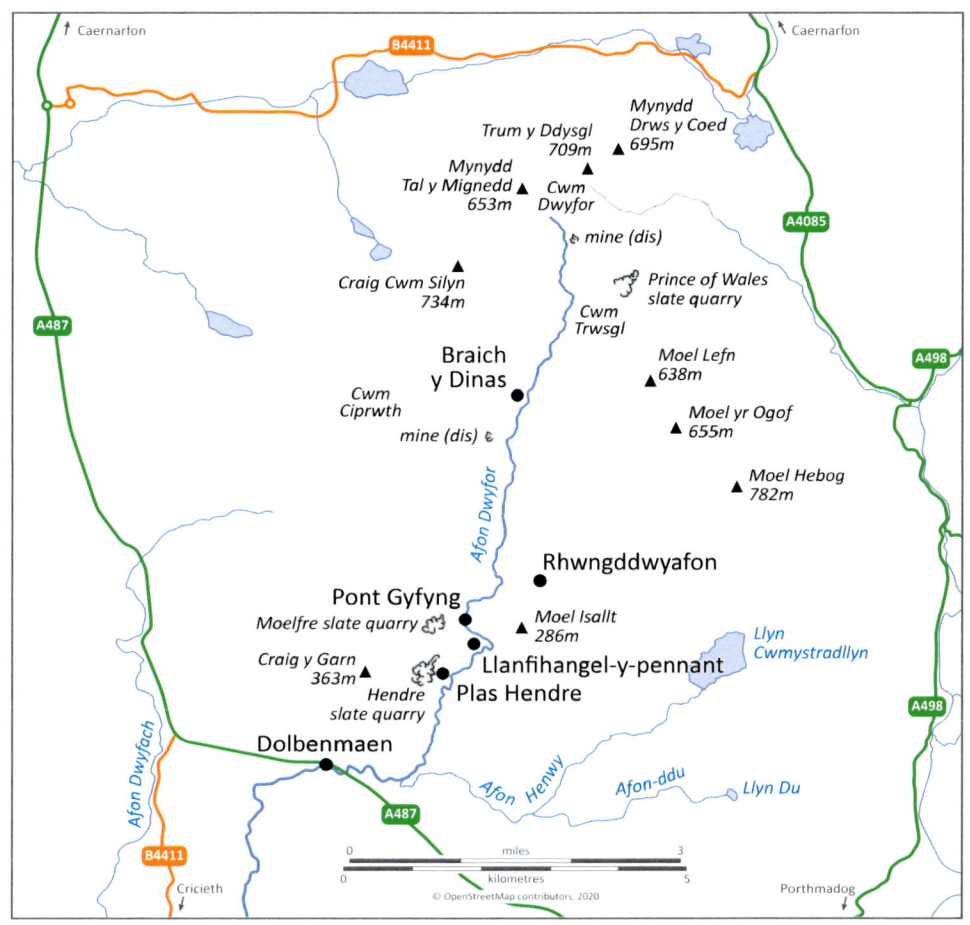

Map of Cwm Pennant

streams entering from the mountains on the east and west of Cwm Pennant. Flowing more or less south west to Dolbenmaen it leaves the National Park and heads briefly west before turning south west again down to Llanystumdwy and thence to the coast. There are two main tributaries, the Afon Henwy emanating from Cwmystradllyn and the Afon Dwyfach that rises not far from Pant Glas on the A487. The river is bridged by roads, paths and not least by the railway line that runs between Pwllheli and Porthmadog.

The estuary is a peaceful place with tremendous views across Tremadog Bay to the Rhinogydd. Criccieth Castle stands proud against the sky a reminder of part of the 'Ring of Iron' set up by Edward I of England. Harlech Castle can also be seen from here. In years past, ships used the estuary as safe anchorage in times of storm. Nothing remains from this time apart from a few rusting stanchions in the boulders by the water's edge. There is no development here so many sea flowers flourish. None more so than thrift. This completely carpets the ground, blanket like, in spring.

The exploration of Cwm Pennant can be undertaken by car although to visit the industrial remains short but steep walks are needed to do this. The Afon Dwyfor, however, is best explored on foot. The section alongside the river upstream from Llanystumdwy is absolutely delightful. Bluebells and wild garlic abound in spring, which along with other flowers such as red campion and ragged robin make this a wonderful place to explore at a leisurely pace on an easily followed path. The section of river downstream of Llanystumdwy is a delight as it becomes tidal to finally flow into Tremadog Bay with a final short lived flourish. There are other walks that can be undertaken although most are shorter. The walk to the source of the Afon dwyfor is steep and is boggy in places. Visits to the mining remains are also steep so again sensible sturdy footwear is advised. The quarries have loose edges so keep well away from these and DO NOT enter any of the adits that are seen. They have long been abandoned and have an abundance of loose rock as well as some deep water. The best map to use is the Ordnance Survey 1:25,000 OS Explorere 254 Lleyn Peninsula East/Pen Llyn Ardal Ddwyreiniol.

Llanystumdwy is the only major

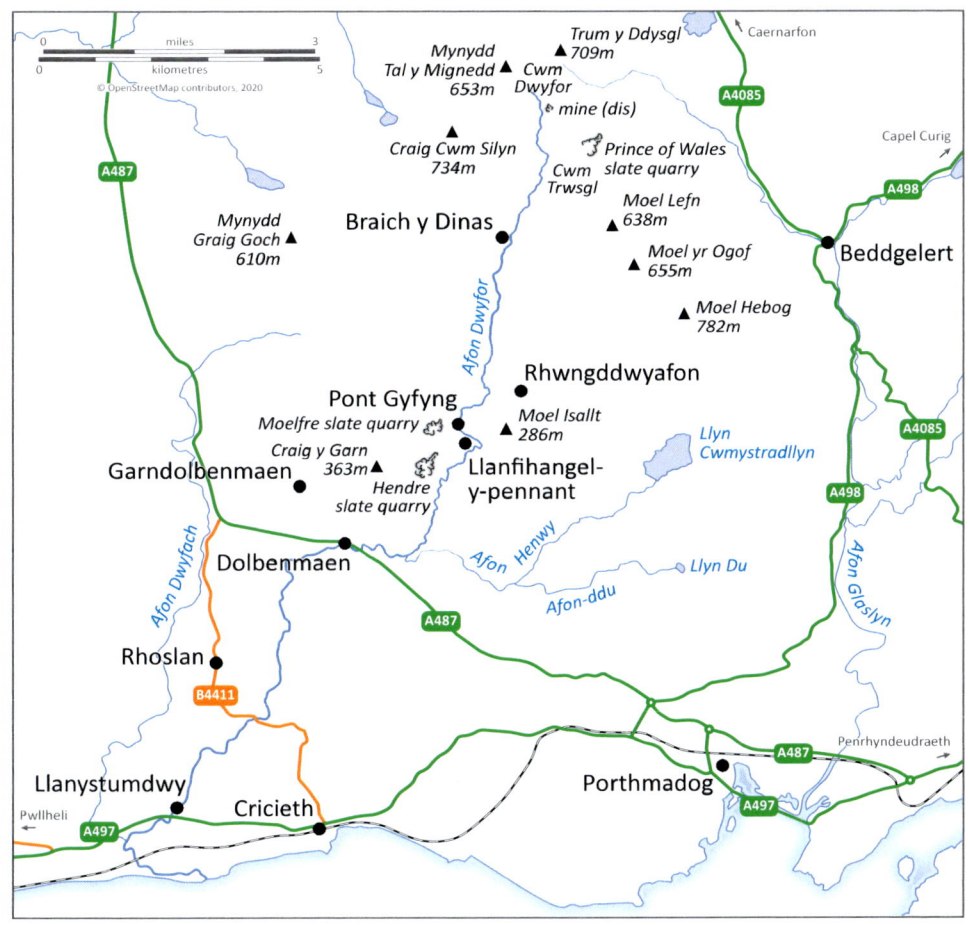

Map of the Afon Dwyfor

habitation along the river. It is famous as being the home of David Lloyd George during his early and later years. He is another of Wales' most famous sons, although he was born in England! There is a museum here along with the house he lived in as a youngster. Called 'Highgate' it is on the main road through the village. He is buried close to the Afon Dwyfor and his grave is easily visited as of course is the museum dedicated to him. Upon retirement from politics he returned to the village to live out his final years and lived at 'Ty Newydd'. This is now the National Writing Centre of Wales. The village is definitely well worth exploring.

Brief notes on some of the walks in Cwm Pennant and along the Afon Dwyfor are included at the end of the book along with a Welsh glossary and of mining terms. Some of these walks are in high mountain terrain so it is important to wear sensible sturdy footwear clothing suited to the current conditions and to be prepared for changes in weather. It can be much colder higher up, even in summer. Take food, water and in cold weather a hot drink. The sun can be strong and the need to cover up is important. Take map and compass, know how to use them although GPS is also a useful tool until the batteries run out! Mobile phone signals are poor in the mountain environment here. That said these walks are very interesting and range high mountain excursions to sylvan, almost level, wanderings at a much lower level. Exploring the area can be accomplished by all at whatever level is appropriate to needs.

For me Cwm Pennant and the Afon Dwyfor are wonderful retreats with no trappings of modern society. There are no man made 'attractions', no quick adrenaline rushes, only peace and tranquillity, of being close to the beauty of nature in all its forms.

Looking down the Cwm Dwyfor incline to Cwm Pennant.

SECTION 1 – SOURCE TO DOLBENMAEN

Chapter 1 – The source of the Afon Dwyfor

Much of upper Cwm Pennant is mountain land with very limited areas of the valley sides suitable for agriculture. As such the more primitive features survive than in lowland areas. Hut platforms from the Dark Ages can be found on the higher mountain slopes. The first people arriving in the valley would have found the area overgrown with trees and scrub making progress difficult. Settlement was undertaken gradually with initial clearings being enlarged as time went by. Only a dozen or so families undertook this venture. Perhaps the first of the modern day settlements occurred around Brynkir during the late 1200's in the relatively sheltered and gradually sloping land and at Isallt in the 1400's which was considered a good *hendref* or winter settlement due its sheltered position. It was on gently sloping ground with smooth slopes and was protected from bad weather from the north by Craig Gyfyng enabling it to enjoy the sunny aspect to the south west.

There are some magical names dotted around the cwm: Rhwngddwyafon - *between two rivers*, Cwm Llefrith - *the valley of milk,* Cwm Sais - *the Englishman's Pass*. These names probably stem from the pioneers who came here to mine the ore and quarry the slate.

House platforms abound along the eastern side of the valley indicating that it was much utilised prior to 'modern man's' exploits to extricate the ore and the stone. It provided a perfect shelter for Iron Age settlers and agriculturalists from the Middle Ages drawn by its abundant timber sources and the constant supply of water. After the timber clearance took place and the ground being even and fertile due to past glacial deposits, it was ideal for settlement and animal enclosure. The sea was also within close proximity and easily accessible for fish, shellfish and seaweed for drying and composting, so with all its attributes this cwm provided the perfect natural and secure enclosure that was needed.

1. Approaching the workings of Cwm Dwyfor copper mine;
2. The wheel pit of Cwm Dwyfor copper mine
3. The Afon Dwyfor flowing through the Cwm Dwyfor incline. This would have been bridged when the mine was operating.

Cwm Pennant and Afon Dwyfor

High above the end of Cwm Pennant is Cwm Dwyfor, a wild unspoilt area. The only sounds are the bleating of the sheep and the rasping calls of ravens. It is a quiet unspoilt place that has returned to what it once was before the ravages of mining and quarrying took place. The remains of these activities are plain to see but have now weathered into the landscape. Although the Prince of Wales slate quarry is visible from afar the copper mine in Cwm Dwyfor is virtually invisible until the cwm is entered. Here the Afon Dwyfor is born and quickly grows into a sizeable stream, ready for its headlong swoop down to the floor of Cwm Pennant.

Beyond the ruins of the mine a wall can be seen traversing the cwm above the mine workings, almost directly under the summit of Mynydd Tal-y-mignedd 653 metres or, in English the '*Mountain at the end of the Bog*'. That is true as there is much swampy ground in Cwm Dwyfor. The summit itself is crowned with a tall stone tower. This was erected by the quarry workers to commemorate Queen Victoria's Diamond Jubilee in 1897. The right arm of the cwm is the long grassy ridge leading up to Trum y Ddysgl, 709 metres, '*the Ridge of the Dish*'. I suppose the hollow of Cwm Dwyfor can be likened to a huge dish or bowl.

Heading up the cwm towards the wall crossing it at mid height the stream becomes significantly smaller but no less steep to where a trickle of water commences just below the wall. This is the start of the Afon Dwyfor's 12½ miles (20.1 kilometres) journey through Cwm Pennant and on to the sea.

In its lower reaches the river becomes good for sea trout and records an annual catch of over 500. Fishing rights on the river are largely managed by the Criccieth, Llanystumdwy and District Angling Association which was formed in 1927. It owns fishing rights on 8 miles of double and single bank fishing and also leases about 2-3 miles of water on the Afon Dwyfor and Afon Dwyfach. Membership of the association, however, is only open to persons residing within 3 miles of the waters which it controls and limited to 160. The association issues day, week and season permits for visiting anglers with concessionary permits for senior citizens

Blaen-pennant with Mynydd Tal-y-mignedd and Trum y Ddysgl beyond.

and full time students. Junior permits up to the age of 16 years are also available.

At the start of its journey numerous streams from Moel Hebog 782 metres and Mynydd Graig Goch 610 metres swell the flow. It initially flows south west to Dolbenmaen and out of the National Park. After briefly heading west it turns south west once again down to Llanystumdwy. from where it continues lazily to the coast. Its mouth has been diverted eastwards by almost a mile by the Penychain shingle spit that resulted from long shore drift.

The principal tributaries are the Afon Henwy, emanating from Cwmystradllyn, joining the Dwyfor just above Dolbenmaen and the Afon Dwyfach which joins just west of Llanystumdwy. This has its source just west of the A487 not far from Pant Glas. The river is bridged not only by the A487 and A497 main roads and the B4411 but also by minor roads and paths as well as the railway line from Cricieth to Pwllheli,. The Afon Dwyfor is perceived as *'the big holy river'* whilst Afon Dwyfach is *'the little holy river'*. *Dwy is the Welsh for God.*

The estuary is now a peaceful haven with many stunning flowers in summer and birdlife. Years ago ships used the deep channel to shelter. There are no signs of this nowadays just a few rusting stanchions on some of the rocks by the water's edge. It remains undeveloped. Part of the Llyn Coastal Path runs alongside the estuary.

Back in Cwm Dwyfor the infant stream tumbles steeply down to reach the cwm floor and flows languidly through the workings of the Cwm Dwyfor copper mine before becoming steep again to cascade to the valley bottom at the head of Cwm Pennant. Mining had been taking place here since 1820 but work was suspended due to the lack of capital. The Mining Company of Wales took possession in 1850 and changed the name of the mine from Blaen Pennant to Cwm Dwyfor. This company too had severe financial pressure. In 1868 a new company called Cwm Dwyfor Copper and Silver Lead Mining Company leased the property. Many of the Directors were also key figures in the nearby Prince of Wales slate quarry, run by The New Prince of Wales Company. Extravagant claims were made of the amount of copper ore to be found so development continued.

Transport was a real headache, a major hurdle and was costly. As a result The New

1. *The source of the Afon Dwyfor;*
2. *Dôl Ifan Gethin and Dolgarth slate quarry;*
3. *Dolgarth slate quarry;*
4. *Blaen-pennant ruin from the tramway to Cwm Dwyfor.*

Prince of Wales Company bought the whole of the Gorseddau Tramway for £5,000 in 1871 the deal being confirmed in 1872. An extension of just over 5 miles was built to the Prince of Wales slate quarry of just over 5 miles from the Braich y Big, or Bib, junction in Cwmystradllyn to the slate mill in Cwm Trwsgl. Here the line split again and went east up the inclines to the slate quarry and west to the Cwm Dwyfor copper mine. This link was completed in 1876, making Cwm Dwyfor the only copper mine in Snowdonia to have a direct rail connection with a port, Porthmadog, courtesy of this extension. Unfortunately the Cwm Dwyfor Copper and Silver Lead Company were very seriously in debt so the mine closed in the same year!

The copper that had been found was of reasonable quality but far from pure as it occurred with marcasite, a low grade iron ore. The line was reopened in 1877 under the Cwm Dwyfor Mining Company Limited and supposedly carried 34½ tons of lead ore, the last recorded output. The mine was abandoned in 1879. One of the finest features of the remains is the huge wheel pit. This housed a wheel of 10.67 metres by 1.22 metres although the housing itself is 12.5 metres by 1.75 metres. Other remains include a crusher house and an incline. This is easily seen and ascended on the approach walk into Cwm Dwyfor.

To the east of the ruined buildings under a line of small cliffs is a terrace of ruined barracks. Here men stayed during the week and returned home at the weekend only to return early on Monday morning to resume their work. There is a covered shaft on the floor of the cwm. The whole tramway system was out of use by the1890's. Today the line is traceable from the foot of the Cwm Dwyfor incline, the Prince of Wales mill and Gorseddau slate quarry all the way to Penmorfa. After Penmorfa it follows a lane before descending the steep craggy slope behind Tremadog via a reversing spur. It then crosses the road to follow the track-bed of the Tremadog Ironstone Tramway. In Porthmadog it follows the present day streets to the port.

Downstream from the ruins the feature at the head of the incline are the remains of a drum or winding house. The

Cwm Dwyfor from the tram-road with Mynydd Tal-y-mignedd as a back drop.

incline bridge over the Afon Dwyfor half way down the incline has long since disappeared and the now quite large stream flows through as it tumbles steeply down to the valley floor. At the base of the incline the tramway contours across the hillside to the Prince of Wales slate mill. Part way along it the spoil heaps of the quarry are easily seen up to the left situated under the sombre, vegetated and broken cliffs of Moel Lefn 638 metres. The mighty Nantlle Ridge is seen on the skyline over to the right.

Approaching the Prince of Wales workings from the remains of the slate mill the obvious feature seen from below is the long incline in between the spoil heaps linking five levels. Below and right of the main workings is the reservoir that supplied water for powering the mill situated 37 metres lower and 350 metres away at the junction of the Gorseddau Junction and Porthmadog Railway.

The mill only processed slate slab. Roofing slates were fashioned in the *waliau* or dressing sheds on the levels. The mill is adorned with some wonderful arched doorways. Close to the mill are the remains of the launder pillars. Like Gorseddau slate quarry the Prince of Wales quarry was a terrible failure. It was vigorously worked between 1863 and 1868 with much investment and growth. A large mill was built that housed four saws and two planers. The waterwheel providing the power was a massive 9.14 metres by 1.22 metres. Until the tramway reached the mill the finished product was transported by packhorse over Bwlch Ddwy-Elor and to Rhyd Ddu and Caernarfon. This was a severe financial burden and the catalyst in extending the Gorseddau Tramway. The opening of the line was on the 12th June 1875 and carried passengers. In 1873 claims of 5,000 tons of slate being produced were made from a workforce of 200 men. In 1875 there was a catastrophic rock fall. As such the company never recovered from the financial cost of dealing with the damage. This forced closure in 1877. However, the last recorded output was in 1886 when it finally closed for good but sporadic working continued right up until 1920.

For such an unsuccessful venture the site is well worth a visit as there is a great deal of interesting remains. There are five

Cwm Pennant from the tram-road.

The barracks at Cwm Dwyfor copper mine.

levels some building remains but the highlight is the fine series of *waliau* on level five. These are opposite the barracks so the men did not have far to go for their work! The barracks did not have family accommodation. Directly behind the reservoir, itself an interesting feature in that it has a double wall with a gap in the middle, are the remains of a workshop. The gap in the dam wall would have been filled with clay and the construction allowed for the dam to be raised when required.

At the end of the tarmac road where the valley levels out are picnic tables, a wonderfully quiet place to contemplate. In spring the slopes on the eastern side just a few metres up the hillside is an amazing display of bluebells, one of the best in Snowdonia. Immediately downstream of the obvious ford here is a wonderful example of a clapper bridge. Across the ford is the solitary ruin of the obvious Dol Ifan Githin. Beyond are ruins of farm buildings but further up the valley on this side are the ruins of Blaen Pennant. Life must have been very hard for the people living here. The ground around it is boggy and very acidic, unsuitable for agriculture.

The scar of Dolgarth Quarry rises above the farm ruins just beyond Dol Ifan Githin. This quarry was worked on three levels with the extracted rock taken down the obvious incline to the left of the workings to the water powered mill at its base. It opened in the 1870's but by 1880 production had ceased. Looking across to this quarry from the opposite side of the valley gives a great view showing how the workings were carried out from the terraces otherwise known as galleries and how they were connected to the incline leading down to the mill area.

1. *Cwm Dwyfor looking towards the source of the Afon Dwyfor;*
2. *The plaque above the door of 'Highgate'.*

Cwm Pennant and Afon Dwyfor

Chapter 2 – Other slate quarries in Cwm Pennant

Although the Prince of Wales slate quarry was the largest in the valley there were other undertakings of notable size. These were developed for convenience of obtaining localised slate for building. Close to Pont Gyfyng and above it in the woodland above are the remains of Moelfre slate quarry. This was developed in the 1860's on earlier workings that had also seen trial mining for copper. Quarried slate went first of all through a cutting then a tunnel before being up-hauled to an adjacent mill. The finished slate was then taken down the hillside to the valley floor via an incline. Taking the slate out of the valley proved to be very expensive forcing closure in the early 1870's. A new lower tunnel provided access as well as drainage enabling the slate to be taken down a new incline to a valley floor mill which used waterpower. The waterwheel pit remains as do the launder pillars beyond it. Around 30 men produced around 600 tons per year. Final closure came about in 1880 but sporadic quarrying continued until the 1930's. Other remains can be seen on the walk up to Cae Amos bothy. Above the main quarry is a notable circular stone structure. This was probably used as a powder house. The bothy, Cae Amos, is a former climbing hut being used as such for 50 years but has now been taken over and renovated by the Mountain Bothies Association and is available for use, free of charge, to all outdoor enthusiasts. Originally it was a hill farm of two storey construction and is around 200 years old. Further down the valley opposite St Mary's church in Llanfihangel-y-pennant is Isallt quarry. This is clearly seen from the churchyard. Isallt was worked between the 1840's and 1850's. Little remains apart from the spoil heaps, some ruins and an incline.

Further down the valley is Hendre Ddu. The early 19th century workings were

The infant Afon Dwyfor close to Beudy Ddol at the end of the tarmac road in Cwm Pennant.

The clapper bridge across the Afon Dwyfor close to end of the tarmac road in Cwm Pennant.

developed further in the 1860's creating a steam mill and an incline to the road. Although 60 men were employed the annual amount produced hardly reached 1,000 tons. Being somewhat un-profitable the mine closed. In 1872 quarrying re-commenced but beset with numerous problems such as the dam collapsing in 1875 but somehow they managed to persevere until 1898 when it failed. A rail link to Cricieth had been planned but the line was never built.

There are some fascinating remains here. Not least are the barracks. These have unusually tall windows and there are vestiges of the dressing sheds. On the left of the access track is the huge pit of the quarry. Below the quarry is the mine manager's house. Called Plas Hendre it is a grand house which today has holiday cottages in part of it.

So what is slate? It is a metamorphic rock which means it has been altered from its original composition. It began forming around 500 million years ago in Snowdonia during the Cambrian period. Originally depositions of fine sediments of clay minerals flaky in character formed a mudstone. Minerals in this determined the colour the slate was eventually going to become. For example the slate above Bethesda and Nantlle tends to have a purple tinge to it, whilst around Blaenau Ffestiniog and Corris as here it is blue grey and is much finer grained. Generally it is slate from the Cambrian period that provides the most durable and hardest slate. Depositions continued over several million years and huge pressures turned the mudstone into shale.

Continued pressure and great heat caused a chemical change to occur. The original clay minerals broke down to become other minerals such as mica and

Dolgarth slate quarry above Blaen-pennant.

feldspar. These were the main constituents of this reformed and different rock now known as slate. Interestingly the minerals had reformed at an angle to the bedding planes. This was the line of cleavage

Nowadays slate is used for a plethora of tourist souvenirs but there have been many other uses. The best snooker tables had slate beds. Other uses apart from roofing slate were, building material, walling, slate plank fencing, flooring, sills, lintels, quoins. It was used to form vats in both the chemical and brewing industries on account of its impervious nature. Cisterns, sold as 'flat packs', were manufactured. In farming it was used in pig sties and cowsheds, dairies and larders not to mention the Victorian 'privy' or Gents toilets. It was also used for making coffins, some of which were re-usable (probably for pauper burials) and gravestones. Slate was also used in the electricity trade where it was used for switchboards and insulation.

1. Remains of the Prince of Wales slate mill with Moel Hebog forming the backdrop;
2. The Prince of Wales slate mill and launder pillars with Cwm Pennant beyond;
3. Looking up to the Prince of Wales slate quarry from the top of the incline above the mill; 4. Bluebells above the road end in Cwm Pennant.

I have included a list of traditional slate sizes for amusement and it can be seen that their names are predominantly 'female'. Sizes are in inches.

Empress 26 x 16
Princess 24 x 14
Duchess 24 x 12
Small Duchess 22 x 12
Marchioness 22 x 11
Broad Countess 20 x 12
Countess 20 x 10
Small Countess 18 x 10
Viscountess 18 x 9
Wide Lady 16 x 10
Broad Lady 16 x 9
Lady 16 x 8
Small Lady 14 x 8
Narrow Lady 14 x 7
Double 12 x 6
Single 10 x 5

Many other sizes and names existed with over 30 being known at the end of the 19th century. 'Queens' could have been anything from 30" x 18" to 36" x 26" or even larger. 'Princesses' were often termed 'Fourteens'. 'Putts' were 14" x 12" sometimes called 'Headers' and 'Ladies Putts' were 13" x 10", 'Damp Course' slates came in many sizes from 20" x 9" down to 9" x 4½".

Dressing sheds, waliau, with Cwm Pennant beyond at the Prince of Wales slate quarry.

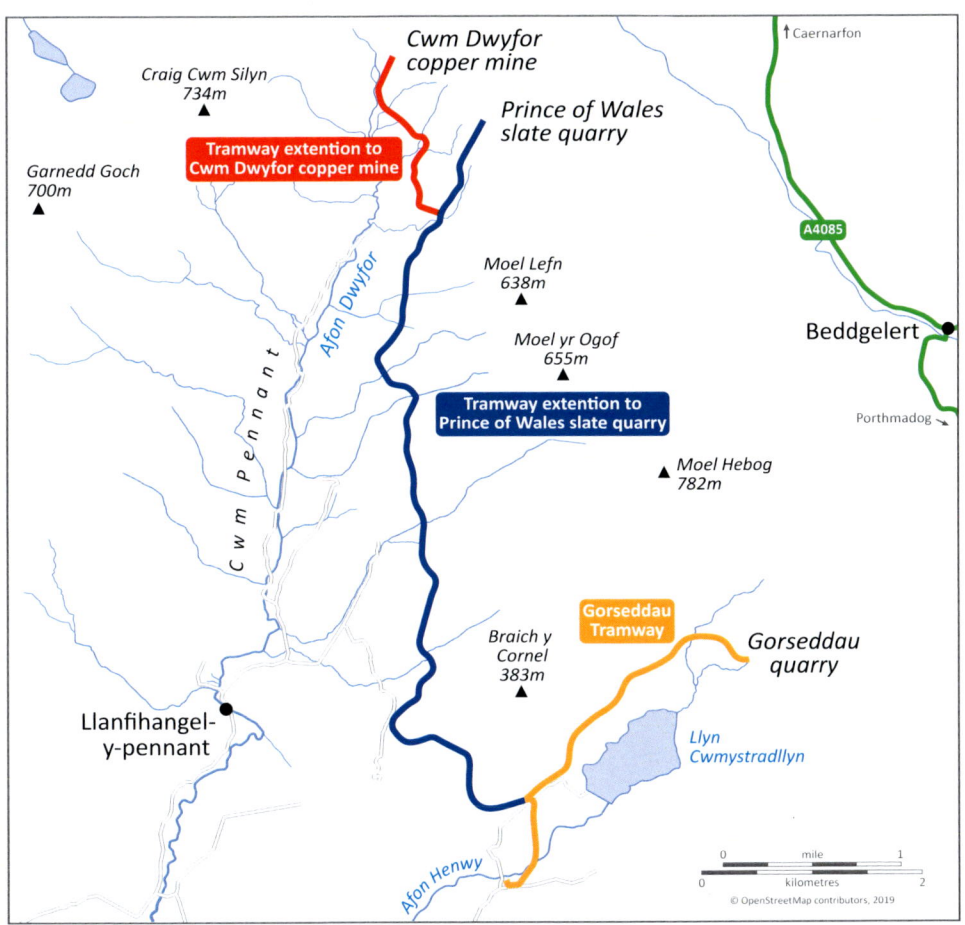

Map of the Gorseddau Tramway

Chapter 3 – Cwm Ciprwth copper mine

The site is on a plateau above Cwm Pennant on the shoulder of Garnedd Goch 700 metres (2,297 feet), one of the mountains forming the Nantlle Ridge. Fortunately the scrap-man must have considered the Cwm Ciprwth site too remote to bother with, which could account for the survival of the waterwheel and other artefacts. The site was extensively restored some years ago by the Welsh Development Agency and Snowdonia National Park. Since then time has taken its toll and the two long flat rods, which had snapped, were replaced in August 2013.

It seems likely that the mine operated in conjunction with Gilfach, passed on the way up to Cwm Ciprwth, and that all ore, etc passed out through the Gilfach adits. The evidence of mining on the site consists of 2 flooded vertical shafts and a horizontal, also flooded, adit. There is an almost complete lack of mining waste or spoil which seems to mean that Cwm Ciprwth was no more than a pumping and access site for Gilfach. In 1828/29 some 40 tons of copper ore were sold. After a lapse in production Gilfach produced 25 tons in 1854. Production ceased shortly after until the Brynkir Gold Exploration Syndicate formed in 1889. By 1890 twelve men worked underground with another 6 above. In 1891/92 that number halved. The mine was liquidated in 1894.

The most notable feature at Cwm Ciprwth is the water wheel, a unique survivor of water power being used for both pumping and winding. It was devoid of noise and pollution. The wheel is complete except for the metal buckets and leat that supplied water to it. This can be traced on the hillside behind but the final section, consisting of presumably a wooden launder, is absent. The water wheel was made by Dingey and Son of Truro, whose name appears several times on the metalwork. The diameter is 8 metres and dates from 1889/90. Presumably the wheel arrived at Cwm

The Cwm Ciprwth copper mine waterwheel.

Ciprwth as a kit of parts as access by anything larger than a horse would seem impossible.

The water wheel drove a pump and a winding drum by means of three flat rods. These are long pieces of straight timber raised above the ground. It should be borne in mind that because the flat rods are not under tension they have bowed somewhat with age. The supports where the flat rods joined each other are hinged at ground level. As the water wheel turned the whole length of the flat rods would move backwards then forwards. This movement was transferred to the pump, which is also hinged at the bottom. The water in the drainage shaft was sucked up by the pump and fed into a channel and then into the stream which flows through the site. At the other end of the pumping mechanism is a counterweight, a box filled with rubble. The winding mechanism on the water wheel consists of a drum operated by a large gear wheel. To engage the drum there is a clutch, although the handle to operate this has been broken off. Presumably the winding mechanism would have been used to access the two flooded vertical shafts, in which case a simple form of pit head gear would have been present.

There are two stone buildings on the site, one consisting of three rooms. This may well have been the smithy, storeroom or miners barracks. The other is a simple square structure next to the stream,

possibly used as an explosives store.

Close to Cwm Ciprwth at road level is Y Gilfach which in the early 1800's was the largest farm in the valley at 829 acres. The present house stands ¼ mile above the Afon Dwyfor in a sheltered nook on the rocky hillside overlooking hay fields and the best pasture in this

*1 The waterwheel at Cwm Ciprwth;
2. The waterwheel and pump mechanism at Cwm Ciprwth. Moel Hebog is to the right with Moel yr Ogof and Moel Lefn to the left;
3. Looking up Cwm pennant from the walk to Cwm Ciprwth. Snowdon is in the background and the Prince of Wales Slate Quarry is seen on the grassy slope right of centre.*

Cwm Pennant and Afon Dwyfor

part of the valley. It is probably situated on the site of an earlier dwelling. The first record is in the second half of the 16th century. Gilfach sheep are still marked with a letter K after the Knight family of the 18th century. Downstream again is Plas y Pennant the owner of which in 1631 also owned Dol Ifan Githin.

1. The swimming area at rhe start of Cwm Ciprwth walk; 2. Remains of a drum-house at Moelfre slate quarry; 3. Launder pillar close to valley floor below Moelfre state quarry; 4. Moelfre slate quarry;
5. Remains of the powder house above Moelfre slate quarry;
6. Ruins at Moelfre slate quarry.

Cwm Pennant and Afon Dwyfor

Chapter 4 – Llanfihangel-y-pennant, Brynkir, House and Tower

Llanfihangel-y-pennant, (*St Michael's church at the head of the valley*), is a tiny hamlet having a sunny outlook on the valley floor, situated close to a large meander of the river. The ancient ecclesiastical parish church is dedicated to Saint Michael and is a grade II listed building, part of the bishopric of Bangor. Although the present church seen today was built in 1840 another existed here in 1710. St Michael is really not a saint at all but an Archangel. Referenced in the old testament he has been part of Christian teachings since the earliest times. Catholic writings and traditions regard him as being the defender of the church and chief opponent of Satan and assists souls at the hour of death. Mihangel is Welsh for Michael. Nestling close to Craig Gyfyng it is sheltered from northerly weather. Across the river the spoil heaps of Isallt slate quarry are easily spotted.

This tiny hamlet has a sunny outlook on the valley floor and is situated close to a large meander of the river. Nestling close to Graig Gyfyng it is sheltered from northerly weather. As previously mentioned across on the eastern side of the valley the spoil heaps for Isallt slate quarry are easily spotted.

Brynkir Tower was originally a folly built as a celebration of the personal success of Sir Joseph Huddart, a millionaire, of Brynkir House. (Note that the knighted millionaire gave an anglicised phonetic spelling to his 'Brynkir'; the correct spelling is found in the village name, Bryncir) He was knighted in 1821 the same year that George the 4th was crowned king. However, it provided work for the local craftsmen in the slump immediately after the Napoleonic Wars. It has been said that Huddart was knighted for his services to industry as well as mine

1. The river at Llanfihangel-y-pennant just downstream of the road bridge;
2. The road bridge over the river before Llanfihangel-y-pennant.

Cwm Pennant and Afon Dwyfor   39

1. St. Michael's church Llanfihangel-y-pennant and Isallt slate quarry;
2. St. Michael's church, Llanfihangel-y-pennant;
3. Ornate tip of headstone in the graveyard of Llanfihangel-y-pennant church.

Cwm Pennant and Afon Dwyfor

1. Brynkir Tower; 2. The ruined Brynkir Hall; 3. Plas Hendre; 4. Typical shot holes seen at Hendre Ddu.

enterprises. These last were not that successful and he landed himself in dire financial straits. He was a friend of William Alexander Madocks who built the rather more useful Cob at Porthmadog.

Today, having fallen into disrepair and becoming a shell, the six storey *Rapunzel like tower has been restored by its present owner. Rapunzel is the fairy story about a maiden in a tower written by the brothers Grimm.* The floors had collapsed and it was possible to see all the way up from floor to roof. Thankfully CADW, a Welsh Heritage organisation, came to the rescue as the structure was a grade II listed building. The tower is now back to its former glory and is now a holiday let. The views across to Hendre Ddu slate quarry and to Cwm Pennant from the grounds are excellent as is the view towards Moel Hebog.

Robert Wynn was the first to adopt Brynkir as a family name in 1563. James Brynkir is buried in Llanfihangel-y-pennant graveyard having died in 1644. His headstone bears the name Brynkir. At the end of the 19th century the Brynkir Estate collapsed, mainly due to the cost of the upkeep of the place. The mansion house had its heyday in the 16th and 17th centuries. Successive owners built what became a tangle of rooms. As one part became uninhabitable another new wing was built! The walls were built from the rock at Craig Gyfyng. In 'Lost House of Wales' by Thomas Lloyd there is an amazing photograph of Brynkir House although much of what is seen in the photo has disappeared.

The house grew into a monster with many long passages leading to unwanted rooms. The place was abandoned, so the story goes, at a moment's notice! The house remained intact having been so well built and was used to house German prisoners of war at the end of WWI. The still well stocked wine cellar was broken into by the prisoners one night so no doubt they had one hell of a boozy session! The bottles had all been personalised by a glass seal bearing the inscription Brynkir. The final breakup of the Estate which had lasted for 400 years came on the afternoon of Friday 25th April 1930. Today the ruins are hidden in a tangle of trees, bushes and nettles. Close to the ruins is a large stone building that was once the stables for the mansion. Until recently this was the Cwm Pennant Outdoor Centre.

Joseph Huddart owned Brynkir House from 1809 but there are reports that he

1. The ruined Brynkir Hall;
2. Llanfihangel-y-pennant from the side of Moel Isallt;
3. Llanfihangel-y-pennant and the spoil heaps of Isallt slate quarry from Moel Isallt.

Cwm Pennant and Afon Dwyfor

was undertaking repairs in 1812. He introduced a marble chimney piece, a kitchen grate, floors and putting in laths for a ceiling but spent most of his time away from the place living in Highbury Place, London. As well as rebuilding Brynkir House, Huddart undertook the complete development of the demesne, land surrounding the house, and Home Farm. The lower part of the valley was designed as a park and the wild slopes tamed and converted into smooth grassland planted here and there with clumps of trees. By 1823 the low hill above the mansion was crowned with a tower. Rocks on the hillside were cleared and built into fine walls. This created rich pasture land. Trees were planted everywhere both in single rows and in thick groves. These protected the cattle and crops. Farm buildings were also erected. Leats were built to bring water, not only for drinking purposes but also to provide power to small waterwheels that in turn powered the churns and dairies in those farms. Harvests were notoriously bad during the depression immediately after the Napoleonic Wars.

1. Cwm Pennant from Craig y Garn; 2. Moel Hebog and Craig Gyfyng from Craig y Garn; 3. Looking down into Cwm Pennant from Craig y Garn with Moel Lefn and Moel yr Ogof to the right of it. The pointed form of Snowdon is in the far distance; 4. The remains of the ditch at the hillfort on Bryniau'r Tyddyn; 5. Craig y Garn from Tyddyn Mawr Camp.

Cwm Pennant and Afon Dwyfor

SECTION 2 – DOLBENMAEN TO LLANYSTUMDWY

Chapter 5 – Dolbenmaen

Dolbenmaen, literally means *'meadow at head of rock'*. Marking the end of Cwm Pennant Dolbenmaen was the administrative centre, *maerdref*, in Eifionydd until 1239. The community includes the villages of Bryncir, Cenin, Garndolbenmaen, Golan, Llanfihangel-y-Pennant, Penmorfa, Pentrefelin, and the hamlet of Prenteg. A castle motte is located to the south of the village which is thought to have been the residence of Llywelyn the Great until the 1230s, when the court moved to a motte and bailey castle at Cricieth. The castle guarded a ford on the Afon Dwyfor which may have been on the Pen Llystyn (Tremadog) to Segontium (Caernarfon) Roman road. The parish church of St Mary's is a grade II listed building.

The castle mound is 36 metres in diameter and some 6 metres high and can be clearly seen from the road despite the trees. On the flat top there is a vague hint of the long vanished stone buildings. Unfortunately it is situated on private land and impossible to visit. A substantial ditch survives on the west, but on the other sides, the base has been damaged by later walls. The mound is worth a look because the grouping of church, castle and manor house, Plas Dolbenmaen, is both attractive and unusual for Wales. Closely knit villages such as this are rare. A village of bondmen would have been attached to the court to work the Lord's fields, hence the tight cluster of houses around it. This motte and nearby church are the only remnants to mark the site of the Prince's Court in the *maerdref*.

The area known as Eifionydd formed the northern half of the former minor kingdom (or division of land known as a *cantref*) of Dunoding within the Kingdom of Gwynedd. Traditionally it took its name

1. *St. Mary's church, Dolbenmaen;*
2. *Plas Holland, the old rectors house in Dolbenmaen adjacent to St Mary's church;*
3. *An old road sign in Dolbenmaen.*

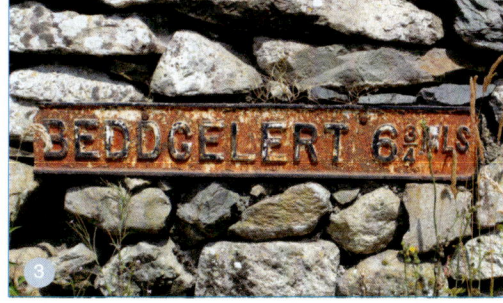

Cwm Pennant and Afon Dwyfor 49

1. The confluence of the Afon Dwyfor on the right and the Afon Henwy;
2. The motte at Dolbenmaen;
3. The Afon Dwyfor between Tyddyn Madyn and Lodge Bridge.

from Eifion, son of Dunod (who gave his name to the *cantref*) and grandson of Cunedda Wledig. Criccieth was the main centre, although there could well have been an earlier royal residence at Dolbenmaen. Whilst it is not a unit of local government, Eifionydd is still in common use for the area which includes the villages of Abererch, Llanaelhaearn, Pencaenewydd, Llangybi, Llanystumdwy, Llanarmon, Rhoslan, Pentrefelin, Penmorfa, Garndolbenmaen, Bryncir and Pantglas. The Afon Dwyfor divides the commot of Eifionydd into two almost equal halves. R. Williams Parry's poem Eifionydd contrasts rural Eifionydd with the bustling slate quarries of Dyffryn Nantlle.

On the bend when entering the village is a very pretty 'wriggly tin' cottage. Just beyond this is a low white bungalow. Until 1964 this was the village sweet shop also selling soap, paraffin and other household commodities.

St Mary's church, a grade II* listed building, originated as a chapelry of St Beuno, Penmorfa. It was built in the 14th and 15th centuries, whilst the bell is dated 1729. The original lych gate was built in 1847. It has been considerably altered at later dates. Now combined as the parish of Dolbenmaen with Penmorfa..The church is a small single cell building constructed with un-coursed local rubble stone with long stone quoins, all of which are partially

Cwm Pennant and Afon Dwyfor

rendered. There is a 19th century slate roof between raised gable parapets. A pointed arch contains the 19th century boarded door having ornamental ironwork. Windows both sides have pointed heads. There is a corbelled gabled bell-cote surmounted by a small stone cross. A slate sundial on the south side of this is of early 19th century vintage.

Interior wise the roof is composed of 5 bays defined by the 15th century arch-braced collar beam trusses with cusped king posts and soffits. These rise directly from the walls. The floor is tiled and the Chancel raised by a single step. Reredos, a screen or wall decoration is at the back of the altar. Three corbels at the west end are probably the remains of beams supporting the west gallery and lit by the high west window. The pulpit is of 19th century vintage of stained wood whilst the altar itself dates from 1931.

North of Dolbenmaen is the alluvial flood plain of the Afon Dwyfor. This continues upstream for a mile or so. To the west of it is good clear, dry ground ideally suited to pasture. To the north west are the bare mountain sides whilst the east slopes of Craig y Garn 363 metres were covered in thick forest that provided timber for the area.

1. & 2. The derelict Plas Dolbenmaen; 3. Brynkir Tower when seen from just below Lodge Bridge.

Chapter 6 – Burial Chambers and a hill-fort

Close to the Afon Dwyfor is the Ystumcegid Isaf Neolithic burial chamber. Found at SH 498413 it is easy to reach from the footbridge just beyond Tyddyn Cethin caravan park and some 600 metres due east away from it. It consists of the remains of a chambered long cairn and dates to the Neolithic period, 4,500 to 2,500 B.C. A long cairn is a roughly rectangular or trapezoid mound of stone, usually between 25 metres and 120 metres long it exceeds twice its greatest width. The mound may have been edged by a timber or stone revetment and contain one or more stone or wooden burial chambers.

The site of National importance, consists of a megalithic chamber having the remnants of a passageway and an associated cairn. The chamber itself is an irregular quadrilateral formed of five upright stones supporting the capstone some 1.2 metres above ground level. It measures 4.8 metres long and 3.5 metres wide and slopes down to the north. The remains of the passageway lie north of the chamber built into a recent field wall. It is defined by three low upright stones and a fourth which is now fallen. This is 1.8 metres long. The cairn material consists of a turf covered stone extending 10 metres to the south and 5 metres into the north of the chamber. A dry stone revetment wall prevents material falling into it. The cairn itself is overlaid with loose boulders and by a field wall which is built through the chamber following the line of the passageway. These monuments help in our understanding of prehistoric burial and ritual practises.

Although situated slightly further afield and not that associated with Cwm Pennant or the Afon Dwyfor this burial chamber can be found at Rhoslan on the B4411. Being so close to a road and on the edge of the village it is worth visiting as it is only a 5 minute walk away across a field starting from the Cricieth end of the village. It has a very impressive capstone.

1. Ystumcegid Isaf burial chamber;
2. The footbridge near to Ystumcegid Farm; 3. Pont Rhyd-y-benllig.

Cwm Pennant and Afon Dwyfor 55

Cefn Isaf burial chamber at Rhoslan.

One wonders how on earth it was lifted into position.

Prior to the Neolithic period was the Mesolithic. During this time the inhabitants of Britain were hunter gatherers. Around 4,000 B.C. migrants started to arrive from central Europe They brought new ideas with them that lead to the transformation of society and landscape. The Neolithic period was characterised by the adoption of agriculture and less arduous pursuits that had previously been undertaken. As much of the land was covered in trees a period of deforestation took place in order to create land that could be farmed. This started to dramatically and permanently transform the landscape. During this period new types of stone tools requiring greater skills were produced and new technology such as polishing were discovered.

During the Neolithic period a wide variety of monuments were built of which many were megalith in nature. (A megalith is a large stone that was used to construct a structure or monument, either alone or together with other stones. Megalithic describes structures made of such large stones without the use of mortar or concrete). The earliest of these are the 'Chambered Tombs' built during the early part of the Neolithic period.

A chambered cairn consists of a fairly large usually stone chamber over which was a cairn. Some chambered cairns are also passage graves. Usually the chamber will contain a large number of internments and situated close to a settlement and served as the community graveyard.

Below are some definitions of the various types of burial chambers -

Passage grave - This has a narrow passage made of large stones.

Chambered tomb - These are covered by earth

Chambered cairn - A chamber covered by stones

Dolmen (**Cromlech**) - These usually only have a single tomb chamber covered by a flat capstone

Barrow (**Tumulus**) - This is a rounded earth mound used during the Bronze Age that covered a burial

Long Barrow - These date to the Neolithic period and are long mounds covering multiple chambers

Cairn - This is basically just a pile of stones covering a burial chamber.

1. An old green lane above the footbridge beyond Tyddyn Cethin caravan site close to Ystumcegid Isaf burial chamber; 2. Ruins of an old farm close to the footbridge beyond Tyddyn Cethin caravan site; 3. River scenery upstream of Pont Rhyd-y-benllig and Tyddyn Cethin caravan site; 4. Pont Rhyd-y-benllig.

1. River scenery upstream of Pont Rhyd-y-benllig and Tyddyn Cethin caravan site; 2. River scenery below Pont Rhyd-y-benllig; 3. Gateway leading from the track close to Pont Rhyd-y-benllig down to the river.

Cwm Pennant and Afon Dwyfor

Close to Dolbenmaen is Craig y Tyddyn Camp, a prehistoric hill-fort. There are two sites within the area. The first is a small fort on top of a rocky ridge and the second a settlement at the foot of the ridge containing the remains of two round huts and a length of walling.

The fort on Bryniau'r Tyddyn immediately to the west of the A487 occupies the western end of a ridge above Tyddyn Mawr Farm. It has grass-covered stone walls on the north, south and east sides which fall steeply away.

Iron Age hill-forts in Wales started being constructed around 700 B.C. and continued until around 60 A.D. This last date coincided with the local Celtic tribes having been subdued by the invading Romans. Most communities then settled down under Roman rule. Hill-forts were

1, 2. River scenery between Pont Rhyd-y-benllig and Llanystumdwy; 3. The 'bedd' of David Lloyd George.

62 *Cwm Pennant and Afon Dwyfor*

constructed mainly for defence. It is odd that these fortification seemed to have no water as well as not being used for permanent habitation. They were, however, designed to withstand small attacks but were more likely built to deter invaders and could also have been used for tribal gatherings, a meeting point for the local tribes that gave them a chance to show off their power. The larger the fort the less likely they would have been attacked.

1. and 2. River scenery between Pont Rhyd-y-benllig and Llanystumdwy; 3. A story tellers seat by the river; 4. River scenery between Pont Rhyd-y-benllig and Llanystumdwy.

Cwm Pennant and Afon Dwyfor

Chapter 7 – The middle reaches of the Afon Dwyfor and Llanystumdwy

The quiet village of Llanystumdwy is of great interest. In English it translates to *the church on the bend of God's river*. The village is well worth a visit, not only for political historians and lovers of fine listed buildings, but also those who love woodland and river scenery. Coed Trefan is a wonderful wood with the Afon Dwyfor flowing through and makes for a very pleasant, gentle walk. Llanystumdwy was by-passed in 1984 by the A497. This straight section of road avoids the narrow road through the village. Llanystumdwy is famous because of David Lloyd George, a former British Prime Minister, and the last Liberal Party leader to be Prime Minister. He lived here until he was 16 and returned to live his final years. His grave in the village was designed by architect Sir Clough Williams-Ellis, creator of the Italianate village of Portmeirion. He also designed the village chapel, Capel Moriah, directly opposite the entrance gates into the museum. A plaque above the gate into Lloyd George's 'bedd' was inscribed by Welsh artist Jonah Jones with a poem written by Lloyd George's nephew Dr William George, a former Archdruid of Wales.

The poem is a form of poetry in strict metre called an 'englyn' and found on many headstones in Wales.

Y maen garw a maen ei goron, - yw bedd
Gwr i'w bobl fu'n wron;
Dyfrliw hardd yw Dwyfor lon
Anwesar bedd yn gyson

W. R . George

Translated the poem reads -
This rough stone crowns the grave
Of a man who was gallant for his people;
The colourful waters of the merry Dwyfor river
Always embraces where he lies

Lloyd George picked up his political nous and hatred of the land-owning aristocracy from his lay preacher uncle. The art-deco

The road bridge over the Afon Dwyfor Llanystundwy.

Lloyd George Museum, another of Williams-Ellis' creations, is also in the village and features artefacts from the politician's life, an audio-visual theatre and a Victorian schoolroom. It is also licensed to conduct weddings. A footpath leading past Lloyd George's grave follows a circular riverbank route through the very attractive Coed Trefan deciduous woodland initially alongside the Afon Dwyfor.

Lloyd George was one of the great reforming British chancellors of the 20th century and Prime Minister from 1916 to 1922. He was born in Manchester on 17 January 1863 the son of a schoolmaster. His father died when he was young whereupon his mother took him to Wales to be raised. He became a lifelong Welsh

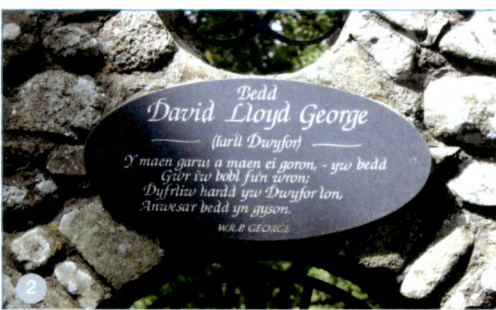

66 *Cwm Pennant and Afon Dwyfor*

1. The 'bedd' of David Lloyd George; 2. The plaque at the 'bedd' to David Lloyd George; 3. The plaque outside the David Lloyd George Museum commemorating the TV series 'The Life and Times of David Lloyd George'; 4. 'Highgate', Llanystumdwy.

nationalist. Qualifying as a solicitor he was elected the Liberal Member of Parliament for Caernarfon in 1890 and held his seat until 1945! He quickly became known for his radicalism and earned notoriety for his opposition to the Boer War.

Below are some notable dates associated with Lloyd George -

In 1905, the prime minister, Sir Henry Campbell-Bannerman, appointed Lloyd George as president of the Board of Trade.

In 1908, he was appointed as Chancellor of the Exchequer in the government of H H Asquith. He then embarked on a period of social reform, the first stage of which was the provision of 5 shillings a week paid to single pensioners. It was known in Wales as 'Coron Lloyd

1. The carved initials of David Lloyd George on the downstream parapet of the bridge spanning the Afon Dwyfor in the village of Llanystumdwy; 2. Date carving on the downstream parapet of the bridge spanning the Afon Dwyfor in the village of Llanystumdwy; 3. The Afon Dwyfor in flood.

George' A *coron* (crown) was 5 shillings. He remained Chancellor through the early years of World War One.

Lloyd George's 1909 budget has been called the 'people's budget' since it provided for social insurance that was to be partly financed by land and income taxes. The budget was rejected by the House of Lords. This, in turn, led directly to the Parliament Act of 1911 by which the Lords lost their power of veto. He introduced the National Insurance Act also in this year. As such he could be said to be the founder of the welfare state.

In 1915 he was appointed Minister of Munitions in Asquith's wartime coalition government.

In July 1916 he became Secretary of State for war, but became increasingly critical of Asquith.

In December 1916 he became Prime Minister, replacing Asquith, with the support of the Conservative and Labour leaders. Lloyd George's achievements in the last two years of the war included persuading the Royal Navy to introduce the convoy system and the unification of the Allied military command under the French General Ferdinand Foch.

Once the atrocities of the war had ceased he was Britain's chief delegate to the Paris Peace Conference that drafted

the Versailles Treaty. Although he remained prime minister Lloyd George was now dependent on Conservative support.

In 1921 he secured the settlement that established the Irish Free State.

1. Ty Newydd, Llanystumdwy, the house where David Lloyd George spent the last year of his life; 2. St John's Church, Llanystumdwy.

In the summer of 1922, Lloyd George was involved in a scandal involving the selling of knighthoods and peerages. In October, the Conservatives withdrew from the coalition over their opposition to Britain's foreign policy in Turkey whereupon he resigned as Prime Minister. Although he stayed in Parliament he was marginalised politically.

In 1944 he was made Earl Lloyd George of Dwyfor.

He died on 26 March 1945 at Ty Newydd, Llanystumdwy, Wales.

Ysgol Llanystumdwy, the village school where Lloyd George received all of his education (he never attended college or university) is still offering primary education to 4–11 year olds, run as a Welsh-medium school under the auspices of the Church in Wales. Close by is St. John's church which dates back to the 19th century.

The Rabbit Farm is an attraction for local families with young children and visitors alike.

The village has a football team, C.P.D Llanystumdwy FC and play in the Gwynedd League.

The local inn, Tafarn y Plu, (also known in English as "The Feathers"), is the last remaining inn of five that once graced the village. It has been open for 200 years and together with its quaint interior has earned itself a place in the book Heritage Pubs of Wales, published by CAMRA. It has long associations with the late playwright Wil Sam Jones.

The village of stone houses is largely an architectural conservation area that has several listed buildings. These include Lloyd George's former residences, his childhood home of Highgate now part of the Lloyd George Museum and Tŷ Newydd, nowadays home to the National Writers' Centre for Wales, established in 1990. The institute or village hall known as Neuadd y Pentref was financed by Lloyd George with compensation he received having won a libel case.

The three-arched bridge (over the Afon Dwyfor) in the centre of the village dates from the late 17th or early 18th century and is Grade II listed. It is claimed that the initials D LL G carved clearly into the downstream bridge parapet are the work of David Lloyd George himself. A former clothes washing place with steps leading down to it, forms part of the river bank immediately upstream of the bridge. The bridge is often mistaken for Bont Fechan. This spans the Afon Dwyfach, a mile away towards Pwllheli close to a garden centre of the same name. The bridge in Llanystumdwy was built in two stages.

1. *Riverside walk scene;*
2. *Capel Moriah in Llanystumdwy.*

When first built the early bridge was only 2.95 metres wide but in 1780 it was widened to 4.9 metres. The join is very evident when seen from under the bridge. An easy walk from the church end of the bridge leads in a few metres to the underside, but do not attempt this when the river is running high!

Tŷ Newydd, a grade II* listed building, built in the 15th century. It was owned by David Lloyd George from 1942 until his death. Prior to that he had asked for his bed to moved to the library where he died! The centre specialises in residential creative writing and retreats with courses in both English and Welsh language covering many genres, forms and styles. It also holds regular seminars and forums. The house has 6 bedrooms, a large dining area, kitchen, conservatory and two libraries. The outbuilding called Hafodty is the tutor's quarters and there are six extra rooms for guests. Inside the house is a fine architectural feature known as a Chinese Chippendale balustrade. The grounds overlook Cardigan Bay and were re-styled in the 1940's by Sir Clough Williams-Ellis.

Close by is Plas Gwynfryn. Once a majestic building it is today a very sad, derelict ruin. Looking up at the house it became quickly apparent that the larger tower is about to collapse. A stone window lintel on the first floor has buckled and cracked with a bulging mass of stone above it is likewise ready to collapse and bringing with it much of the tower above.

Plas Gwynfryn is mentioned as being in existence in the 16th century and owned by Gruffydd ap John ap Grono. It came into the Wynn family in the 17th century then to the Ellis family. In 1866 the old house was replaced with the castellated style building seen today.

The tower, is as much of the house, is built with brick but with a stone outer and was built by Hugh John Ellis-Nanney and completed in 1876 (with a date stone on the tower). He was also the village squire, a Tory and Anglican. He dominated the Nonconformist, poverty stricken population. This made an indelible impression on David Lloyd George who was later to name Llanystumdwy *'the blackest Tory Parish in the land'*. Plas Gwynfryn remained a family home until 1928, just a mere 52 years, before it became a retirement home for the clergy, then a hospital and finally a hotel. This mixed history is not uncommon in the life of grand structures such as this. It was gutted

The collapsing remains of Plas Gwynfryn

by fire in 1982 and has remained derelict ever since. A sad end to a once grand building. However, a squatter took up residence for a brief period before being evicted, with the notion and very ambitious but futile idea to restore the building to its former glory! The only remains of his tenure was an easy chair and radio!

Sadly, Plas Gwynfryn remains a very depressing sight. Any attempt at restoration would need a very deep well of money as well as much TLC. I find it so sad that what was once an, obviously, opulent building has deteriorated into the decayed wreck it is today.

SECTION 3 – LLANYSTUMDWY TO THE SEA

Chapter 8 – To the sea

After rushing through Llanystumdwy the Afon Dwyfor becomes much more benign and pursues a languid approach to the sea. Many trees line the banks until the tidal section of the river is reached. Trees become absent but *Spartina Grass* grows prolifically in the estuary. It is a tall grass and has flower stalks resembling wheat. It has thick, wide leaves with a strong and complex root system. It's more common name is 'cord grass'. It is considered to be an invasive species as it suffocates other estuary plants. as well as destroying the mudflats which are an important feeding ground for the estuary birds. The grass also grows near fresh water. In late summer another invasive, alien species, of plant is found, Himalayan Balsam. Although it has very attractive flowers it reproduces prolifically.

In early summer the banks of the river are a carpet of pink thrift, other flowers such as red campion, ragged robin, bird's foot trefoil and sea holly can all be found. The Coastal Path misses out the tree fringed section of river and joins it below the point in which it becomes tidal. This is the true left of the river. Continuing downstream the path passes some large boulders at the water's edge. These have metal rings that at one time would have been used for boats to berth. The Coastal Path crosses a boggy section thankfully on a boardwalk after which the path continues to the point where the Dwyfor finally disgorges into Tremadog Bay. On the true right of the river the tree fringed section ends at the point where the river becomes tidal. Over to the right is the incredibly exposed Ty'n y Morfa. This solitary house must be a pretty wild place to stay especially during gales. The sound of the sea crashing close by must be very stimulating.

The railway line crosses a fine bridge at the point where the river becomes tidal, not far below the confluence with the Afon Dwyfach. Construction of the railway

The view to the Rhinogydd from the true left bank.

between Aberystwyth and Pwllheli began in 1861 after an Act of Parliament had been passed in that year. It was known as the Aberystwyth and Welsh Coast Railway. Porthdinllaen close to Nefyn was going to be the northern terminus of this Cambrian Coast line because at one time it was going to be the main port for Ireland. In the event this did not come to be because Holyhead was chosen instead and the line terminated at Pwllheli. Initially construction of the line began from Machynlleth, the then terminus of the railway line from Shrewsbury to Aberystwyth. This section was completed in 1864.

The building of the line from Machynlleth to Barmouth was not without difficulties. In fact these were huge, not least the building of the bridge across the Afon Mawddach at Barmouth and the high level length of track above the cliff close to

Fairbourne and, of course, the bridge itself. Two incidents have occurred on the line when engines plunged down the cliff from the high level section fortunately leaving the carriages on the line! One occurred in 1883 and the other in 1933 which unfortunately killed the train crew on both occasions.

In 1867 the line was extended to Pwllheli via Porthmadog. At that time Aberystwyth was spelt Aberystwith. The new spelling started being used in 1892. Porthmadog was spelt Porthmadoc at that time as well. Before the railway line was built the river downstream of the bridge was used for small boats. Closer to the sea the river channel becomes quite deep. The river gives a little lively flourish as it ripples noisily over shingle into the bay and the end of its journey from the mountains. It has been called one of the loveliest rivers in Snowdonia if not in Wales. It is often overlooked in favour of the more well known rivers such as the Glaslyn, Mawddach, Dyfi and Teifi. A visit will not disappoint.

1. Looking downstream from just below the A487 at Llanystumdwy; 2. Sea Holly.

The views across Tremadog Bay to the Rhinogydd on the far skyline are spectacular as is the view towards Cricieth and its Castle standing proud above the town. Criccieth is regarded as an anglicised form of Cricieth the Welsh spelling. However, it is generally accepted nowadays with a double c. Cricieth was settled in the Bronze Age and there is evidence that Celtic people lived here around the 4th century B.C. The castle was built by Llwelyn ap Iowerth in 1230 although not recorded as such until 1239 when presumably it was completed. In 1282 as part of the newly conquered lands the castle amongst many others in Wales belonged to Edward 1. On the 16th September 1400 Owain Glyndwr launched a revolt against the English after being

Cwm Pennant and Afon Dwyfor

80　*Cwm Pennant and Afon Dwyfor*

declared a traitor by Henry IV and was proclaimed Prince of Wales. By 1403 there was huge support for the cause and Cricieth Castle fell in the spring of 1404. It was torn down, sacked and burnt. In 1284 Cricieth became a borough after being granted a charter by Edward 1.

The town began to grow again from the backwater it had become in the 19th century due to greatly improved transport

1. Looking towards the Rhinogydd from the true right bank; 2. Reeds, Llanystumdwy and Moel Hebog; 3. Looking upstream towards Yr Eifl (The Rivals); 4. The Moelwyns, Cricieth and Moel y Gest.

links. The turnpike road from Tremadog through the town was created in 1807. On a natural note there is a very unusual flower here that was introduced in the 19th century by a resident of Min y Mor. It is called the Oxenbould Daisy (*lampranthus roseus, rosy dew plant*). It is an evergreen, has pink flowers and grey/green foliage. It is bushy, compact and forms a rounded cushion.

1. and 2. Anchorage fixings on the river bank close to the estuary. 3. At journeys end, the point where the river meets the sea; 4. Canada geese.

Chapter 9 – Walks to discover the area

To appreciate the area further a selection of short walks follows. The walks to Cwm Dwyfor and Prince of Wales slate quarry have a common start at the head of Cwm Pennant. Although not very long they are in mountainous terrain. Walks to Cwm Ciprwth copper mine, Moelfre and Hendre Ddu slate quarries although short are quite steep. Likewise the walks up Craig y Garn and Moel Isallt, again short, have a short steep section. The others are gentle rambles alongside the gently flowing Afon Dwyfor. One of the prettiest walks in the area is the walk upstream alongside the Afon Dwyfor starting in Llanystumdwy whilst the walk downstream from Bont Fechan is an absolute delight when the riverbank is lined with a carpet of pink thrift.

All the walks follow paths, tracks or roads that are rights of way.

Walk 1 - *Cwm Dwyfor copper mine.*
Starting from the small fee paying car parking area at the head of Cwm Pennant this walk follows the way-marked path up to a ruin and over a ladder stile. It then turns left and follows the much degraded tramway to the incline leading up into Cwm Dwyfor. The return walk reverses the outward one.

Walk 2 - *Prince of Wales slate Quarry.*
Start as for the previous walk up to the ruin and turn right along a path that leads to the remains of the once grand mill and the start of the linking tramway from Gorseddau. Going uphill from the mill the drum house at the top of an incline is reached and the expanse of the Prince of Wales quarry is spread out in front. A path wanders through and around the workings to the top of them before returning down a broad ridge to the ruin by the ladder stile and thence back to the car parking area.

Walk 3 - *Cwm Ciprwth copper mine*
Although only a mile, including the return, this walk is quite a steep one to reach the mine area to view the remains of this remarkable site. However, it is well worth seeking out. The site feels very remote yet it is so close to the road down in the valley. It starts at a layby on the left immediately before the gate spanning the Afon Dwyfor at SH 532476. There is a way-marked wooden gate on the left of the layby. Follow the closely spaced marker posts to Cwm Ciprwth.

Walk 4 - *Moelfre slate quarry.*
The walk to Moelfre slate quarry is again quite short but steep. It starts close to Pont Gyfyng where there is a widening in the road. Crossing the river it follows an access track at first then a signed path to the left of a house to reach a track. A short way up this is another track going off and up to the right. This is followed past workings and ruins to where the large tree filled quarry is reached. A peculiar small circular stone building is seen up to the right. The walk here is on the path leading to Cae Amos a mountain bothy further up. There are fine views of Moel Hebog.

Walk 5 - St Mary's church in Llanfihnagel-y-pennant is only a few hundred metres stroll. It starts at the road bridge of Pont Gyfyng. There is a wide layby here where 2 or 3 cars can be parked. Walking back across the bridge a small wooden gate is seen on the left. Pass through this and follow a path to another gate to reach the church.

Walk 6 - *Hendre Ddu slate quarry* is easily reached from the minor road up Cwm Pennant up a way-marked rough quarry access track some 550 metres beyond the toll house at the turning for Brynkir. There are good views of the lower reaches of Cwm Pennant.

Walk 7 - *Afon Dwyfor roiver walk.*
The walk from Llanystumdwy to Pont Rhyd-y-benllig is an absolute treat especially when the bluebells are in bloom. Starting from the burial site in Llanystumdwy the wide path wanders gently up and alongside the Afon Dwyfor through the very pretty Coed Trefan to a track close to the bridge. Either return along the track or retrace steps alongside the river - much better! This is a must do walk.

Walk 8 - *Llanystumdwy to the sea and Cricieth.*
From the A497 the road that bypasses Llanystumdwy follow the access road to Aberkin Farm. There is a fisherman's car park at the start of this road. From the farm follow the track down and cross the railway line. The path, part of the Llyn Coastal Path, follows the side of the Afon Dwyfor to where it debauches into the sea. Either return the same way or continue along the signed coastal path into Cricieth.

Walk 9 - *Alternative walk to the sea.*
This walk starts at Bont Fechan a short distance away in the Pwllheli direction from Llanystumdwy almost opposite the cemetery. There is also a small garden centre nearby. A loop of the old road makes a very convenient car parking place. The signed path is followed to where theAfon Dwyfor becomes tidal. Follow the true right bank all the way to the sea. The river bank is lined with thrift and is a sea of pink in spring. There are extremely good views on this walk especially across the bay towards the Rhinogydd.

Walk 10 - *The ascent of Craig y Garn.*
Whilst not in Cwm Pennant itself, but rising above it as a fine shapely looking peak, the ascent of Craig y Garn, 363 metres, from Garndolbenmaen is an absolute delight as the view from the summit is magnificent with much of Cwm Pennant visible. The view also encompasses much of the western side of Snowdonia including Snowdon itself. In summer the bilberries on the hill are prolific.

Walk 11 - *The ascent of Moel Isallt* metres For such a lowly height this walk gives magnificent views from the 286 metres high summit to the head of Cwm Pennant showing off to great effect the huge dish shaped hollow of Cwm Dwyfor. It also has a great view of the lower reaches of Cwm Pennant and its relationship to the sea. The close up view of the massive form of Moel Hebog is superb as is the view of the lower reaches of Cwmystradllyn. The view across to the Nantlle Ridge and Craig y Garn completes the very fine panoramic vista. The quarries of Moelfre and Hendre Ddu in relation to each other is also clearly seen. Llanfihangel-y-pennant is seen to occupy a grassy area beside a large meander in the river. The walk starts at the end of the tarmac road above Brynkir close to Isallt Fawr. After gentle slopes a short but steep climb reaches the summit which is crowned with a low walled shelter.

GLOSSARY

ADIT - A horizontal passage in a mine used for drainage, haulage or access. An adit was also driven for exploratory purposes.

BARRACKS - **Welsh: Baràcs**
The accommodation area used by quarrymen usually through the week but occasionally all year

BACH - Little

BEUDY - Cow shed

BLAEN - Source of a river or head of valley

BRAICH - Promontory

BRITHDIR - Mottled or speckled land

BRON - Hillside

BRYN - Hill

BWLCH - Pass

CAE - Field

CANOL/GANOL - Centre, central

CANTREF/HUNDRED - The largest and principal division of land

CEFN - Ridge

CEGID - Hemlock

COED - Wood

COEDWIG - Forest

COMMOT - Welsh Cwmwd. A secular division of land in Medieval Wales. The subdivision of a 'hundred. There were 2 to 3 commots per hundred. Eifionydd and Ardudwy were commots of Dunoding

COPPER - A soft reddish mineral and used in alloys such as brass and bronze. Symbol Cu

COPPER PYRITES/CHALCOPYRITE - Also known as yellow sulphide of copper because of the combination of copper and sulphur with an equal proportion of iron . A brassy-yellow unaltered ore that has not been exposed to weathering called Chalcopyrite

CRAIG/GRAIG - Rock, crag

CWRT - Court

DINAS - Fort

DÔL - Meadow, Dale

DWY - God

ENGINE SHAFT - A shaft fitted for pumping equipment

FATHOM - Is a measurement of 6 feet and was the miner's unit of depth

FACH - Bend of a river or a nook

FFRIDD - Rough mountain land or moorland

FLAT RODS - Iron rods that were 20 feet long and linked together to transmit power from a waterwheel or rotating engine to the pumping shaft

FECHAN/FYCHAN - Vaughan

GARN/CARN - Cairn
GARREG/CARREG/CERRIG - Stone, rock
GWELY - Bed
HAFOD - Summer dwelling
HENDRE - winter settlement
ISAF - Lowest
LAUNDER PILLARS - These pillars were built from stone and were used to support a trough, often wooden, that allowed water to be conveyed to a waterwheel or for the buddles
LEAT - An artificial watercourse or aqueduct dug into the ground, especially one supplying water to a mill or waterwheel
LEVEL - A horizontal passage in a mine and used for drainage haulage, ventilation or access
LLAN - Originally this meant an enclosure but nowadays it pertains to church, usually of a saint
LODE - A vein or rake of mineral in a fissure
MAEN - Rock, stone
MAES - Square (in a village or town)
MAWR - High, great, big
MELIN/FELIN - Mill
MÔR: Sea
MOEL/FOEL - Bare hill or hilltop
MOTTE - An early form of castle introduced by the Normans. It consisted of a large mound of earth on top of which was a wooden tower
MYNYDD/FYNYDD - Mountain
PENNANT - Head of the stream or valley
PLAS - Mansion
PONT/BONT - Bridge
SHAFT - A vertical or nearly so opening into a mine. They were used for a number of purposes that included access, winding or hauling out the ore and ventilation
TRUM - Ridge or crest
TRWSGL - Clumsy
TŶ - House
TYDDYN - Small holding, small farm
UCHAF - Highest
WALIAU - Open fronted slate dressing sheds
WEN/GWYN - White
WERN/GWERN - Swamp, marsh
YSTUM - Bend

COMPACT CYMRU
– MORE SNOWDONIA TITLES:

www.carreg-gwalch.cymru

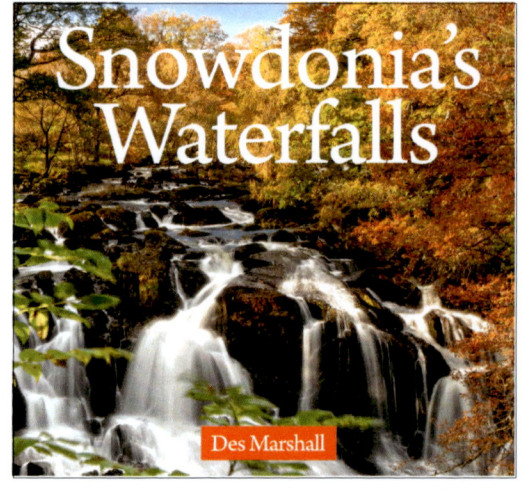

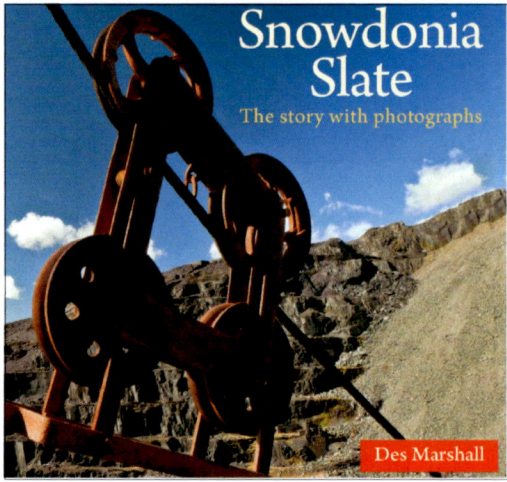